IØ177653

TOPIC

Are You Ready To Get to the Other Side?

SCRIPTURES

1. **Mark 4:35-41** — On the same day, when evening had come, He said to them, "Let us cross over to the other side." Now when they had left the multitude, they took Him along in the boat as He was. And other little boats were also with Him. And a great windstorm arose, and the waves beat into the boat, so that it was already filling. But He was in the stern, asleep on a pillow. And they awoke Him and said to Him, "Teacher, do You not care that we are perishing?" Then He arose and rebuked the wind, and said to the sea, "Peace, be still!" And the wind ceased and there was a great calm. But He said to them, "Why are you so fearful? How is it that you have no faith?" And they feared exceedingly, and said to one another, "Who can this be, that even the wind and the sea obey Him!"

2. **1 Peter 1:7-8** — That the genuineness of your faith, being much more precious than gold that perishes, though it is tested by fire, may be found to praise, honor, and glory at the revelation of Jesus Christ, whom having not seen you love. Though now you do not see Him, yet believing, you rejoice with joy inexpressible and full of glory.

3. **Hebrews 11:24-27** — By faith Moses, when he became of age, refused to be called the son of Pharaoh's daughter, choosing rather to suffer affliction with the people of God than to enjoy the passing pleasures of sin, esteeming the reproach of Christ greater riches than the treasures in Egypt; for he looked to the reward. By faith he forsook Egypt, not fearing the wrath of the king; for he endured as seeing Him who is invisible.

SYNOPSIS

The five lessons in this study *Giant, It's Time For You to Come Down!* will focus on the following topics:

- Are You Ready To Get to the Other Side?
- Are You Willing To Be Interrupted by Compassion?
- Are You Ready To Kill the Giants in Your Life?
- Are You Using the Weapons of Love?
- Is Complaining the Giant in Your Life?

The emphasis of this lesson:

When Jesus told His disciples they were going to the other side of the Sea of Galilee, He meant it. You may have a dream or desire from God of what He has called you to do, and there might be obstacles you face along the way. But just like Jesus in the boat with the disciples, *you* are going to the other side regardless of those obstacles. Although your situation may seem impossible to navigate, God is with you, and He will do what He has promised!

Jesus' Faith Enabled Him To Be Unmoved in the Storm

Jesus' life is an example of how we are to live — including how to walk in overcoming faith and how to experience the peace of God. We see this clearly in the gospel of Mark where Jesus is journeying with His disciples to the other side of the Sea of Galilee. After teaching the crowds multiple parables, Mark tells us:

> **On the same day, when evening had come, He [Jesus] said to them, "Let us cross over to the other side." Now when they had left the multitude, they took Him along in the boat as He was. And other little boats were also with Him.**
> **— Mark 4:35-36**

First, it is important to note that when Jesus said, "Let us cross over to the other side," He was not just making a suggestion or filling time and space with words. He meant exactly what He said — He and His disciples were going to the other side of the lake.

If God has spoken something to you through the Scriptures or by His Spirit, He is going to do it! Whether it's a dream of operating in some type of ministry or an assignment to birth a new business, what God has spoken to you, He will fulfill as you yield to and cooperate with Him.

A Note From Denise Renner

The Word of God is so powerful in our lives. It is essential that every person spend time with God and study His Word in order to stay spiritually strong in these last days.

This study guide corresponds to my *TIME With Denise Renner* TV program by the same title that can be viewed at **deniserenner.org**. My desire is that through these lessons, you find the encouragement and freedom in Christ that you need. I believe the Holy Spirit is going to speak to you through the words you read in this study tool and that as you begin to use it, you will be *propelled* into the abundant life God has planned for you. I encourage you to make the effort to receive all He has for you and all He wants to do in you — it will definitely be worth it!

Whether you have walked with the Lord a long time or have just begun to follow Him, there is so much He wants to give you from His Word. He sees where you are, and He wants to meet you there.

> Therefore do not worry about tomorrow, for tomorrow
> will worry about its own things.
> Sufficient for the day is its own trouble.
> — Matthew 6:34

Your sister and friend in Jesus Christ,

Denise Renner

Unless otherwise indicated, all scripture quotations are taken from the *New King James Version®*. Copyright © 1982 by Thomas Nelson. Used by permission. All rights reserved.

Scripture quotations marked (*AMPC*) are taken from the *Amplified® Bible*. Copyright © 1954, 1958, 1962, 1964, 1965, 1987 by The Lockman Foundation. Used by permission. **www.Lockman.org**.

Scripture quotations marked (*NKJV*) are taken from the *New King James Version®*. Copyright © 1982 by Thomas Nelson. Used by permission. All rights reserved.

Giant, It's Time for You To Come Down!
Overcoming Faith Is Yours

Copyright © 2025 by Denise Renner
1814 W. Tacoma St.
Broken Arrow, Oklahoma 74012-1406

Published by Rick Renner Ministries
www.renner.org

ISBN 13: 978-1-6675-1252-5

eBook ISBN 13: 978-1-6675-1253-2

All rights reserved. No portion of this book may be reproduced or transmitted in any form or by any means — electronic, mechanical, photocopy, recording, scanning, or other (except for brief quotations in critical reviews or articles) — without the prior written permission of the Publisher.

Of course, that doesn't mean you won't have obstacles. Shortly after Jesus got into the boat with His disciples, the Bible goes on to say:

> **And a great windstorm arose, and the waves beat into the boat, so that it was already filling. But He [Jesus] was in the stern, asleep on a pillow....**
> — **Mark 4:37-38**

Notice that despite the great windstorm and the boat filling up with water, Jesus was immovable and undisturbed. In fact, He was so wrapped up in the peace of God and in faith that He was asleep on a pillow while the storm was raging!

The Bible goes on to say:

> **...And they awoke Him and said to Him, "Teacher, do You not care that we are perishing?" Then He arose and rebuked the wind, and said to the sea, "Peace, be still!" And the wind ceased and there was a great calm.**
> — **Mark 4:38-39**

Again, Jesus was undisturbed by the storm, and rather than give in and take on the fear and panic of His disciples, He stood up in faith and spoke peace to the wind and the waves. And the storm obeyed Him!

You Have All the Faith You Need

You may hear that story and think, *I don't have that kind of faith. As a matter of fact, I don't have much faith at all.* That is not true. God said that He has given "a measure of faith" to everyone — including *you* (*see* Romans 12:3). And regardless of how small your faith may seem, you have all the faith you need to still the storm and make it to the place God told you He was taking you!

Although none of us enjoy the trials and troubles we go through, while God never sends them, He will use them to grow and deepen our faith. The apostle Peter describes this in First Peter 1:7-8, telling us:

> **That the genuineness of your faith, being much more precious than gold that perishes, though it is tested by fire, may be found to praise, honor, and glory at the revelation of Jesus Christ, whom having not seen you love. Though now you do not see Him, yet believing, you rejoice with joy inexpressible and full of glory.**

Friend, your faith — the faith that God Himself deposited inside your spirit the moment you surrendered your life to Christ — is *precious* in His sight. It is more valuable than gold, which is one of the most valuable substances on earth, so don't downplay or belittle the faith you have! Jesus said, "…If you have faith as a mustard seed, you will say to this mountain, 'Move from here to there,' and it will move; and nothing will be impossible for you" (Matthew 17:20).

The very fact that you are trusting in Jesus Christ — whom you have *not* seen — and you love Him and believe He is the Son of God who died for your sins and rose from the dead, is proof of your faith. Although you cannot physically see God, Jesus, or the Holy Spirit, by faith you "see" and believe in the Trinity, and that is precious in God's eyes!

Moses operated in this same kind of faith, and the Bible talks about it in Hebrews 11:

> **By faith Moses, when he became of age, refused to be called the son of Pharaoh's daughter, choosing rather to suffer affliction with the people of God than to enjoy the passing pleasures of sin, esteeming the reproach of Christ greater riches than the treasures in Egypt; for he looked to the reward. By faith he forsook Egypt, not fearing the wrath of the king; for he endured as seeing Him who is invisible.**
> **— Hebrews 11:24-27**

Through faith in God — who is invisible — Moses gave up the temporary pleasures of sin and the treasures of Egypt and endured the troubles and trials brought on by the wrath of Pharaoh. And that is what *you* are doing. By faith in God and Christ Jesus, whom you cannot see, you are enduring the trials and troubles this life brings to one day receive the eternal blessings God has promised.

Jesus Stayed in Faith
and Experienced God's Saving Power

Realize that while Jesus was fully God, He was also fully man. That means Jesus faced the same kinds of doubts, worries, and fears that we face and all the same temptations we deal with. Yet He did *not* give in to them and sin (*see* Hebrews 2:17-18; 4:15). He had to live by faith moment by moment, day by day just like we do.

Looking again at Mark's account of Jesus and the disciples in the midst of the storm, the Bible says:

> Then He arose and rebuked the wind, and said to the sea, "Peace, be still!" And the wind ceased and there was a great calm. But He said to them, "Why are you so fearful? How is it that you have no faith?" And they feared exceedingly, and said to one another, "Who can this be, that even the wind and the sea obey Him!"
>
> — Mark 4:39-41

Jesus' faith produced great peace in Him during the storm, and out of that peace arose great authority to stand in faith and speak to the wind and the waves. He did not lose His focus as He was going to the other side of the sea. Even though the disciples were screaming at Him and He was facing a life-threatening storm with them, Jesus stayed in faith and experienced the saving power of God.

You have that same peace and authority inside of you because the Spirit of Christ lives in you (*see* Romans 8:9-11). You can stand in faith and speak to any storm that is raging around you and tell it to be still, in Jesus' name!

There Is Always a Person To Reach on the Other Side of a Storm

It is vital to realize that Jesus was not just out on a boat ride with His best buddies. He had a God-ordained purpose on the other side of the Sea of Galilee. Jesus had an appointment to bring deliverance to a man who was bound by demons. The gospel of Mark describes what happened when Jesus and the disciples made it to the other side:

> And when He had come out of the boat, immediately there met Him out of the tombs a man with an unclean spirit, who had his dwelling among the tombs; and no one could bind him, not even with chains, because he had often been bound with shackles and chains. And the chains had been pulled apart by him, and the shackles broken in pieces; neither could anyone tame him. And always, night and day, he was in the mountains and in the tombs, crying out and cutting himself with stones.
>
> — Mark 5:2-5

Jesus' faith and the leading of the Holy Spirit took Him through a horrible storm to go and minister to this demonized man. At Christ's command, the legion of unclean spirits came out of the man and entered a herd of 2,000 pigs, which then drowned in the sea, leaving the man at peace and in his right mind (*see* Mark 5:13-15). It was the compassion of God that motivated Jesus to cross a raging sea to touch and deliver this one demonized man and forever change his life.

Like Jesus, you, too, are to listen for the leading of the Holy Spirit and minister to those whom He shows you. Whether it is 1 person or 1,000, it takes just as much faith to step out of your comfort zone and minister to someone else. Never underestimate the value of reaching out and helping one person.

Think about what would happen if each of us heard and obeyed the voice of the Holy Spirit. If we would say, "Holy Spirit, I sense Your leading and hear You calling me. I am using my faith now to step out of my comfort zone and go minister to the person You are showing me. Flow through me as You flowed through Jesus to bring the fullness of God to this person in the form of hope, healing, restoration, or salvation. In Jesus' name. Amen!"

People Around You Need God's Healing Touch Through Your Hands

Denise shared a remarkable story of how the Holy Spirit opened her eyes while she was in another country to see a woman in need. This woman was serving in the restaurant where Denise was having breakfast, and she appeared to be hurting and in great pain. Denise explained:

> This woman was serving, but she could barely do her job because she was having so much trouble walking. It was clear from her face that she was suffering and in pain. Nevertheless, she did the best she could with the strength she had.
>
> As I was eating my breakfast, all I could think about was this woman. *I've got to go pray for this lady,* I thought. At the same time, other thoughts bombarded my mind trying to keep me from doing anything. You've probably heard some of these same thoughts yourself:
>
> *What are people going to think if you go over and pray for that woman? Do you really believe that if you pray for her God would*

actually do something? Like bring her healing or perform a miracle? Who do you think you are?

You are always going to have obstacles like this that you'll have to push through. A decision is always required to step out in faith and touch that one person God is laying on your heart.

Finally, after I finished my breakfast, I made the decision to go and talk to the woman. 'What has happened?' I asked.

'Well, I've been to the emergency room four times in the last 48 hours,' she responded, 'trying to get some kind of relief from this terrible pain.'

'Can I touch you and pray for you?' I asked.

'Yes,' she said. 'I was up all night, crying out to God to help me.'

So, I touched her and prayed for God's supernatural power to heal her. I then told her, 'The Bible declares that the healing power of God has gone into you. When Jesus prayed for people like I just prayed for you, He would release His healing power and then ask the person to do something they couldn't do previously. So what have you been unable to do?'

'I've had difficulty walking without pain,' she said as she held onto the edge of the counter.

'Well, why not try to walk right now?'

Immediately, she let go of the counter and started walking.

'Whoa!' she said. 'That's strange. It doesn't hurt as badly as it did.'

You could see on her face that something was different. So, I encouraged her to keep on walking. 'The power of God has touched you!' I declared.

When I came back the next day, that woman's face was just beaming! I watched in amazement as she was walking perfectly normal, carrying everything with ease, smiling at everyone.

'My life has changed!' she said excitedly.

What had changed her life? It was the power of God! His miraculous touch had transformed her life, and that same supernatural power is on the inside of you! If you will just open your heart and mind like Jesus did and go where His Spirit leads you, He will use you to bring life-transformation to those who are hurting.

Jesus Went Through Much Difficulty To Reach One Man

As we said at the opening of the lesson, Jesus' life is an example of how we are to live — including how we are to walk in overcoming faith. We saw that after a long day of teaching, Jesus was moved by the Spirit of God to go to the other side of the sea of Galilee. He got into a boat with His disciples and told them, "We're going to the other side."

Suddenly and unexpectedly, a great windstorm manifested, and the disciples were overcome with fear — believing that day may be their last. As the wind-whipped waves continued to beat against the boat and dump water inside, the disciples woke Jesus from His sleep and said, "…Do You not care that we are perishing?" (Mark 4:38) Jesus then stood up and calmed the storm, and the boat made it safely to the intended destination in the country of the Gadarenes where the man tormented by demons was delivered and set free.

Jesus went through a great deal of difficulty to get to that man, a man that most of us would certainly avoid at all costs. Let's face it, very few Christians would want to minister to a demonized man who was screaming, cutting himself, and living in a graveyard. This man was notorious for being so powerful and violent that he had even broken the chains with which he had been bound. Although this was not the kind of person we would want to walk up to, it is exactly the kind of person Jesus went to. And the Bible says Jesus delivered that man, bringing him into complete freedom.

What's the Purpose in Telling You All This?

Time is short, and we're living in the last of the last days when people are desperate to receive help and answers to the difficulties they're facing. We must learn to yield ourselves to the Holy Spirit and be willing to help others break free from the "giants" they are facing.

Friend, God wants to bring down the giants in our lives and then use us to bring down the giants in other people's lives. If you are willing, begin to pray, "Father, I believe that You are great, and Your Spirit lives inside of me. Open my spiritual ears to hear and obey Your voice. Use me today to help someone else. In Jesus' name. Amen."

Then listen for the Holy Spirit's leading. If He tells you to speak to someone, *do it*. If He tells you to lay hands on someone and pray for them, *do it*. Remember, there are people all around you that are overwhelmed by the worries and cares of this life, filled with fear and confusion over all the insanity that's taking place in the world. They don't know God and they need to learn about Him through you.

Even if you feel afraid, the Holy Spirit will strengthen you to *do it afraid*, because "…Greater is he that is in you, than he that is in the world" (1 John 4:4 *KJV*). If you'll be available and obedient to the Lord, you'll soon see for yourself that the power of God will join you and give you the words to speak and the courage to speak it.

So let's open our mouths and speak the life-giving words of God to those who are hurting! Let's get our hands out of our pockets and lay them on those who need a touch from the Lord. When we do, "giants" are going to come down!

STUDY QUESTIONS

Be diligent to present yourself approved to God, a worker who does not need to be ashamed, rightly dividing the word of truth.
— 2 Timothy 2:15

1. When it comes to talking with others, one of the greatest fears that we struggle with is not knowing what to say to people when God brings them across our path. If that is something you have dealt with, check out His amazing promise to you in Matthew 10:19-20, which is repeated in Mark 13:11 and Luke 12:11-12. How might you take this promise and turn it into a prayer declaration?

2. Denise shared how God prompted her to pray for a woman who was hurting, touching the woman gently as she prayed. What do these examples from Scripture tell you about the relationship between God's healing power and your hands? How do they move you to action?
    • Luke 4:40-41; 13:10-13

- Mark 16:18
- Acts 8:14-17
- Acts 9:17-18; 28:7-9
- First Timothy 4:14; Second Timothy 1:6

PRACTICAL APPLICATION

**But be doers of the word,
and not hearers only, deceiving yourselves.
—James 1:22**

1. Before Jesus and the disciples got into the boat, the Holy Spirit had spoken to Jesus, instructing Him to cross over to the other side of the sea. What has God spoken to you through the Scriptures or by His Spirit? Has He given you a dream of operating in some type of ministry or an assignment to birth a new business? Take a few moments to briefly write down what you believe He's telling you to do. As you yield to and cooperate with His Holy Spirit, He will fulfill what He has said.

2. There is always a person to reach on the other side of a storm. For Jesus, it was the demonized man in the Gadarenes who needed deliverance. Who is God calling *you* to reach? Whose name or face keeps coming up in your mind? Think about how you can pray for them or when you can pay them a visit.

LESSON 2

TOPIC

Are You Willing To Be Interrupted by Compassion?

SCRIPTURES

1. **Mark 5:2-13** — And when He had come out of the boat, immediately there met Him out of the tombs a man with an unclean spirit, who had his dwelling among the tombs; and no one could bind him,

not even with chains, because he had often been bound with shackles and chains. And the chains had been pulled apart by him, and the shackles broken in pieces; neither could anyone tame him. And always, night and day, he was in the mountains and in the tombs, crying out and cutting himself with stones. When he saw Jesus from afar, he ran and worshiped Him. And he cried out with a loud voice and said, "What have I to do with You, Jesus, Son of the Most High God? I implore You by God that You do not torment me." For He said to him, "Come out of the man, unclean spirit!" Then He asked him, "What is your name?" And he answered, saying, "My name is Legion; for we are many." Also he begged Him earnestly that He would not send them out of the country. Now a large herd of swine was feeding there near the mountains. So all the demons begged Him, saying, "Send us to the swine, that we may enter them." And at once Jesus gave them permission. Then the unclean spirits went out and entered the swine (there were about two thousand); and the herd ran violently down the steep place into the sea, and drowned in the sea.

2. **Luke 10:17-18** — Then the seventy returned with joy, saying, "Lord, even the demons are subject to us in Your name." And He said to them, "I saw Satan fall like lightning from heaven."

3. **Luke 13:10-13** — Now He was teaching in one of the synagogues on the Sabbath. And behold, there was a woman who had a spirit of infirmity eighteen years, and was bent over and could in no way raise herself up. But when Jesus saw her, He called her to Him and said to her, "Woman, you are loosed from your infirmity." And He laid His hands on her, and immediately she was made straight, and glorified God.

4. **Luke 7:12-15** — And when He came near the gate of the city, behold, a dead man was being carried out, the only son of his mother; and she was a widow. And a large crowd from the city was with her. When the Lord saw her, He had compassion on her and said to her, "Do not weep." Then He came and touched the open coffin, and those who carried him stood still. And He said, "Young man, I say to you, arise." So he who was dead sat up and began to speak. And He presented him to his mother.

SYNOPSIS

God has placed inside you an overcoming faith that is so powerful you can bring down any "giant" that is coming against you. Anxiety, worry, fear, financial difficulties, and relational struggles are no match for the overcoming power of His Spirit living in you. Indeed, God's Word says, "…Whatever is born of God overcomes the world. And this is the victory that has overcome the world — our faith" (1 John 5:4).

The emphasis of this lesson:

Christ was consistently moved with compassion to heal and deliver people who were oppressed by the devil. God's supernatural compassion will empower you too. It will move you out of complacency and inconvenience and push you past fear and hardship, enabling you to accomplish God's will and do the impossible.

Jesus Demonstrated Overcoming Faith

In Lesson 1, we saw how Jesus operated in faith when He and His disciples found themselves face to face with a life-threatening storm. After a long day of ministry, Jesus and the disciples got into a boat and began to make their way across the Sea of Galilee. But before long, a powerful windstorm arose, creating huge waves and flooding their boat with water.

Much to the surprise of the disciples, Jesus had fallen asleep on a pillow in the stern of the boat. When it seemed that they would be swallowed up by the sea, they panicked and went to Jesus in a frenzy, waking Him up. Scripture says, "…He [Jesus] arose and rebuked the wind, and said to the sea, 'Peace, be still!' And the wind ceased and there was a great calm" (Mark 4:39).

Within a short time, Jesus and His disciples made it safely to the other side of the lake just as He said they would. Their next assignment was to go to a notoriously demonized man in the country of the Gadarenes.

Jesus Was Drawn to People in the Most Dreadful Conditions

We pick up the continuing story in Mark 5, where the Bible says:

And when He [Jesus] had come out of the boat, immediately there met Him out of the tombs a man with an unclean spirit, who had his dwelling among the tombs; and no one could bind him, not even with chains, because he had often been bound with shackles and chains. And the chains had been pulled apart

by him, and the shackles broken in pieces; neither could anyone tame him. And always, night and day, he was in the mountains and in the tombs, crying out and cutting himself with stones.
— Mark 5:2-5

Although it may seem hard to believe, there are people today who are living in the same kind of torment as this man who is described in Mark 5. Denise's husband Rick encountered a demonized person similar to this while going to the barber shop for a haircut. The poor man was so vexed in his soul and spirit that he was screaming uncontrollably.

Can you imagine living in such agonizing conditions as the demonized man in the Gadarenes? Day and night, he cried out and shrieked in torment, cutting himself with stones trying to put himself out of the misery he was in. Not even metal chains and shackles could hold him down.

It's probably safe to say that very few believers would sign up to go minister to an individual overwhelmed by such darkness. Most of us would distance ourselves as far away as possible from such a person. But that is not what Jesus did. He knew of this Gadarene man's dreadful condition, and that is why He persevered through the violent storm to reach that man and deliver him.

Christ was consistently moved with *compassion* to reach out and heal people and deliver those who were oppressed by the devil (*see* Acts 10:38). The more we continue to grow in faith and in the love of God, the more we will be empowered like Jesus and moved with compassion to get out of our comfort zone and help people break free from the clutches of the enemy.

Ministering to the Hopeless and Broken Requires a Decision of the Will

Philip Renner, Rick and Denise's middle son, has a heart to minister to people who are spiritually and emotionally trapped in dark and dreadful places. Frequently, he reaches out to people bound by homosexuality and drugs. In fact, it is not uncommon to find Philip ministering to individuals at a gay pride parade or in a crack house where people are shooting drugs into their veins through hypodermic needles. He has even reached out to those who practice worshiping the dead.

When asked if going into such dark places excited him, Philip answered, "To be honest, many times I have to make myself go into those dreadful places. Although I know in my heart, I am called to minister to these severely broken, hopeless people, I still have to make a decision to actually do it."

Philip went on to tell of a time when he went to a place that was so dark he didn't want to go inside. But as he prayed for God's strength and tried to deal with his conflicting emotions, he suddenly felt the presence of God come on him, and he started weeping with great intensity.

"God's presence was so powerful," Philip said, "I was filled with a super-natural compassion that moved me to go and bring deliverance to those in need. Instead of just feeling sorry for the people, I was filled with a Christlike compassion that drove me out of my comfort zone and feelings of reluctance and into a position of serving where I ministered to the broken and brought them what they needed."

God's Supernatural Compassion Enables Us To Do the Impossible

Jesus was driven by such compassion! Regardless of the powerful wind and waves, Jesus knew He and His disciples had to reach the other side — and when they arrived, Jesus' compassion moved Him to set a man free.

Since the birth of the Church, throughout the centuries many believers have learned to lay down their own life for the sake of the Gospel and continue the Great Commission to seek and save those that are lost and make disciples of all nations.

William Tyndale was such a person. Born in England in 1494, Tyndale became an English Bible scholar and linguist that God used to help bring about the Protestant Reformation. As his devotion to God deepened, the Lord instilled within Tyndale a supernatural compassion that drove him to translate the Hebrew and Greek Scriptures into the language of the common people.

Tyndale endured tremendous persecution from the established religious leaders of his day and was ultimately executed at the age of 41 for what they claimed was heresy — however, he achieved the goal God had called him to fulfill, giving us the first translation of the Bible in English. Aren't you grateful for his Christlike compassion and faith? The Bible you hold today is a result of Tyndale's great sacrifice.

That is what God's supernatural compassion will empower you to do. It will move you out of complacency and inconvenience and push you past fear, hardship, and suffering to achieve what seems to be impossible.

Satan and His Demons Recognize Jesus' Superior Authority

Returning to our story in Mark's gospel, the Bible says, "When he [the demonized man] saw Jesus from afar, he ran and worshiped Him. And he cried out with a loud voice and said, 'What have I to do with You, Jesus, Son of the Most High God? I implore You by God that You do not torment me'" (Mark 5:6,7).

Now this passage reveals something very important. Clearly, these demons, who are the ones talking here, acknowledged Jesus' superior power. So much so that they were *begging* and *imploring* Jesus — whom they recognized as the "Son of the Most High God" — not to torment them.

Make no mistake, the devil remembers the day he got kicked out of Heaven, and every host in the unseen realm remembers it too. The Bible tells us plainly that the 70 disciples Jesus sent out returned with joy because the demons were subject to them in His name (*see* Luke 10:17). Jesus told them:

> **"...I saw Satan fall like lightning from heaven. Behold, I give you the authority to trample on serpents and scorpions, and over all the power of the enemy, and nothing shall by any means hurt you."**
> **— Luke 10:18-19**

The devil and the demons who do his bidding know the all-powerful and authoritative voice of Jesus. And the demons in this Gadaraean man knew Jesus could say the word and they would be thrown out — just as Lucifer was kicked out of Heaven, as fast as lightning. That's why they pleaded with Jesus — because they were terrified of Him.

Jesus Evicted the Enemy and Delivered the Demoniac

At that point, Jesus looked at the Gadaraean man who was kneeling before Him and spoke directly to the demonic spirits inside him, saying:

"...Come out of the man, unclean spirit!" Then He asked him, "What is your name?" And he answered, saying, "My name is Legion; for we are many." Also he begged Him earnestly that He would not send them out of the country. Now a large herd of swine was feeding there near the mountains. So all the demons begged Him, saying, "Send us to the swine, that we may enter them." And at once Jesus gave them permission. Then the unclean spirits went out and entered the swine (there were about two thousand); and the herd ran violently down the steep place into the sea, and drowned in the sea.

— Mark 5:8-13

In that defining moment, the once demon-infested man was gloriously set free! Moved by supernatural compassion and faith, Jesus defeated the devil and delivered a man from the powers of darkness!

And just as the demons trembled in fear at the authority of Jesus, they will tremble in fear when *you* step out in faith into that supernatural place of compassion. Remember, Jesus has given you His authority "...to trample on serpents and scorpions, and over all the power of the enemy, and nothing shall by any means hurt you" (Luke 10:19).

At Times It Was Jesus' Faith
That Brought Healing to People

The Bible documents numerous people that Jesus healed and delivered — including a woman who had been stricken by sickness for many years. Luke's gospel tells us:

Now He was teaching in one of the synagogues on the Sabbath. And behold, there was a woman who had a spirit of infirmity eighteen years, and was bent over and could in no way raise herself up.

But when Jesus saw her, He called her to Him and said to her, "Woman, you are loosed from your infirmity." And He laid His hands on her, and immediately she was made straight, and glorified God.

— Luke 13:10-13

Can you imagine being bent over and in pain for *18* years, unable to stand up straight on your own? That is how this woman had been living. What is interesting about her situation is that it was not her faith that healed her from the infirmity. It was Jesus' faith, moving through compassion, that brought healing to her body when Jesus laid His hands on her. This demonstrates His kind and generous heart.

Moved With Compassion, Jesus Raised a Widow's Son Back to Life

Another example revealing the compassionate heart of Jesus in action involves a widow living in the town of Nain, which was in the southern-most part of Galilee. The Bible says:

> **Now it happened, the day after, that He [Jesus] went into a city called Nain; and many of His disciples went with Him, and a large crowd. And when He came near the gate of the city, behold, a dead man was being carried out, the only son of his mother; and she was a widow. And a large crowd from the city was with her. When the Lord saw her, He had compassion on her and said to her, "Do not weep." Then He came and touched the open coffin, and those who carried him stood still. And He said, "Young man, I say to you, arise." So he who was dead sat up and began to speak. And He presented him to his mother.**
> **— Luke 7:11-15**

On the surface, this must have looked like a normal day to all the onlookers in the town. There was nothing unusual about seeing a funeral procession in the streets. People die every day.

What made this situation so unique is that somehow Jesus knew the young man who had died and was being carried out to be buried was the only son of his mother and she was a widow. So on this occasion…

An interruption of compassion fueled by faith made the ordinary extraordinary.

Think about it. There was a large crowd from the city there showing both great pity and concern for this woman and her dead son. But it wasn't their pity that interrupted the funeral. It was Jesus' compassionate faith.

Notice that verse 13 says, "When the Lord saw *her*, He had compassion on her…." It doesn't say, "When the Lord saw the *casket*…," or "When the Lord saw the *crowd*…." It says, "When the Lord saw *her*, He had compassion on her and said to her, 'Do not weep'" (Luke 7:13). Then Jesus did the unthinkable, the unimaginable — He stopped the funeral and talked to the dead man! "…And He said, 'Young man, I say to you, arise'" (Luke 7:14).

Again, it was not the faith of the widow that raised her only son back to life — it was faith and compassion moving together through Jesus that completely changed the situation.

Be Available and Willing To Bring Healing to Others

Now you may be thinking, *If compassion fueled by faith brings healing, why do we not see more believers stopping funerals and raising the dead? Or walking into a mall or grocery store to touch and heal the crippled?* Some might answer this question by saying, "I'm not Jesus," and even though that's true, He does live inside believers in the person of the Holy Spirit. Again and again, the Bible declares, "…Your body is the temple of the Holy Spirit who is in you, whom you have from God…" (1 Corinthians 6:19).

You have the faith-filled, compassionate One living on the inside of you!

You too can bring the extraordinary to a situation by allowing an interruption of compassion from the Spirit of God to flow through you! It's not a fairytale but a fact — Jesus was and *is* a miracle worker. Just as He walked the earth more than 2,000 years ago healing and delivering people, He is still healing and delivering people today. He hasn't changed. The Bible says that "Jesus Christ is the same yesterday, today, and forever" (Hebrews 13:8). That healing power — that supernatural, compassionate power — is resident on the inside of you, and just as the Holy Spirit directed Jesus where to go and who to pray for each day, He is ready and willing to direct you too.

Friend, it's time for us to embrace the faith God put in us when we were born again. It's time to shine with the love of God and let the lost world around us see that Jesus is alive today and that He lives in us! It's time to recognize the compassion of Jesus on the inside of us and begin speaking His truth — the Word of God — and laying our hands on the sick so they can recover.

Yes, the Holy Spirit is in you so that you can walk in peace and have all your needs met — but He also wants to meet the needs of others *through you*! And because He lives in you, you can draw from His strength and give to others the message of the Gospel, the presence of God, and the power of His Spirit with which they long to be touched. Aren't you thankful that someone reached out to you? Then why not be available and willing to reach out to others, giving them the same life-changing experience with Jesus that you were so blessed to receive!

STUDY QUESTIONS

Be diligent to present yourself approved to God, a worker
who does not need to be ashamed, rightly dividing the word of truth.
— 2 Timothy 2:15

1. How much power and authority does the name of Jesus carry? To help you better understand this all-important truth, check out these eye-opening passages, and write down what the Holy Spirit reveals to you about the matchless supremacy found in the name of Jesus Christ.

    • **Jesus is God, Creator of everything** — John 1:1-3; Colossians 1:15-18; Hebrews 1:1-3

    • **Jesus embodies the fullness of God** — Colossians 1:19; 2:9-10

    • **Jesus is from above and above all** — John 3:31,35

    • **Jesus is far above every rule, authority, and power** — Ephesians 1:18-23

    • **Jesus has the Name above all names** — Philippians 2:9-11

2. God has wired each of us uniquely to be able to effectively reach certain people who are hurting. How do Paul's words in Second Corinthians 1:3-4 help you identify the people God will most likely give you compassion for and call you to minister to?

PRACTICAL APPLICATION

But be doers of the word,
and not hearers only, deceiving yourselves.
— James 1:22

1. Philip Renner, Rick and Denise's middle son, has a heart to minister to those who are spiritually and emotionally trapped in dark and

dreadful places. To whom do you feel most called to minister to? Are you actively reaching out to these hurting people? If so, in what ways?

2. If you're struggling in your faith to reach out to others, pray for God's supernatural compassion to rise up within you and empower you to do His will. Ask the Holy Spirit to touch your heart in such a way that you are moved out of a mindset of complacency and inconvenience and freed from fear — rising above hardship and suffering. As you feed on God's Word and pray, He will enable you to do the impossible.

LESSON 3

TOPIC

Are You Ready To Kill the Giants in Your Life?

SCRIPTURES

1. **1 Samuel 17:28-37** — Now Eliab his oldest brother heard when he spoke to the men; and Eliab's anger was aroused against David, and he said, "Why did you come down here? And with whom have you left those few sheep in the wilderness? I know your pride and the insolence of your heart, for you have come down to see the battle." And David said, "What have I done now? Is there not a cause?" Then he turned from him toward another and said the same thing; and these people answered him as the first ones did. Now when the words which David spoke were heard, they reported them to Saul; and he sent for him. Then David said to Saul, "Let no man's heart fail because of him; your servant will go and fight with this Philistine." And Saul said to David, "You are not able to go against this Philistine to fight with him; for you are a youth, and he a man of war from his youth." But David said to Saul, "Your servant used to keep his father's sheep, and when a lion or a bear came and took a lamb out of the flock, I went out after it and struck it, and delivered the lamb from its mouth; and when it arose against me, I caught it by its beard, and struck and killed it. Your servant has killed both lion and bear; and this uncircumcised Philistine will be like one of them, seeing he has defied the armies of the living God." Moreover David said, "The Lord, who

delivered me from the paw of the lion and from the paw of the bear, He will deliver me from the hand of this Philistine." And Saul said to David, "Go, and the Lord be with you!"

2. **1 Samuel 17:42-46** — And when the Philistine looked about and saw David, he disdained him; for he was only a youth, ruddy and good-looking. So the Philistine said to David, "Am I a dog, that you come to me with sticks?" And the Philistine cursed David by his gods. And the Philistine said to David, "Come to me, and I will give your flesh to the birds of the air and the beasts of the field!" Then David said to the Philistine, "You come to me with a sword, with a spear, and with a javelin. But I come to you in the name of the Lord of hosts, the God of the armies of Israel, whom you have defied. This day the Lord will deliver you into my hand, and I will strike you and take your head from you. And this day I will give the carcasses of the camp of the Philistines to the birds of the air and the wild beasts of the earth, that all the earth may know that there is a God in Israel.

3. **Proverbs 23:7** — For as he thinks in his heart, so is he....

4. **Revelation 22:4** — They shall see His face, and His name shall be on their foreheads.

SYNOPSIS

God has given you a race to run, but the enemy does not want you to win, and he will bring everything he can against you to try to stop you. Offense and unforgiveness, bitterness and negativity, and fears of all kinds are just some of the devices Satan will use to trip you up and stop you from achieving your purpose.

Thankfully, God has equipped you with His Spirit and all the spiritual weapons you need to enforce Christ's victory over a situation. His ability through you empowers you to be unstoppable in the pursuit of His will for your life. In this lesson, we will look at the life of David and see how God enabled him to overcome all kinds of obstacles and defeat the giant that was taunting and intimidating the people of Israel.

The emphasis of this lesson:

David was a man after God's own heart. Despite the opposition he faced from his family and those in authority, he trusted in the faithfulness of the Lord. Before going into battle, he pictured himself obtaining

victory over the giant and spoke it out by faith. Then, David defeated Goliath in the name of the Lord, using only a sling and a stone.

When Saul Was Rejected, David Was Selected

The story of David begins in First Samuel 16. At that time in Israel's history, Saul was ruling as king, but because he had disobeyed the Lord repeatedly, Saul had been rejected by God. Shortly after, the Lord found another to take Saul's place. David was that man — a man after God's own heart (*see* Acts 13:22).

God spoke to the prophet Samuel and instructed him to stop mourning over Saul. God then told him to go to the house of Jesse in Bethlehem where he would find the one God had chosen to be Israel's next king. In those days, Samuel's notoriety was equal to that of a country's president! Therefore, when he arrived in Bethlehem unannounced, it was a big deal, and "...the elders of the town trembled at his coming..." (1 Samuel 16:4).

Samuel met with Jesse and his sons, consecrating them and inviting them to join him in making a sacrifice to the Lord. The Bible says, "So it was, when they came, that he looked at Eliab and said, 'Surely the Lord's anointed is before Him!'" (1 Samuel 16:6) But before Samuel could anoint Eliab, God told him plainly:

> ...Do not look at his appearance or at his physical stature, because I have refused him. For the Lord does not see as man sees; for man looks at the outward appearance, but the Lord looks at the heart.
>
> — 1 Samuel 16:7

One by one, Samuel evaluated each of Jesse's sons as they were brought to him. After Eliab, Abinadab was brought before Samuel. Next was Shammah, followed by Jesse's four remaining sons. "Thus Jesse made seven of his sons pass before Samuel. And Samuel said to Jesse, 'The Lord has not chosen these.' And Samuel said to Jesse, 'Are all the young men here?' Then he said, 'There remains yet the youngest, and there he is, keeping the sheep.' And Samuel said to Jesse, 'Send and bring him. For we will not sit down till he comes here'" (1 Samuel 16:10-11).

When David was brought in, the Lord immediately spoke to Samuel and said, "'...Arise, anoint him; for this is the one!' Then Samuel took the horn of oil and anointed him in the midst of his brothers; and the Spirit of the Lord came upon David from that day forward..." (1 Samuel 16:12-13).

God Sees All the Makings of a Mighty Warrior in You

Even though we don't know all the dynamics of David's relationship with his father and his brothers, there is one thing that seems to be clear. In his father and his brother's eyes, David was an *afterthought*. The fact that Jesse didn't think to include David with his brothers from the time Samuel asked him to gather *all* his sons is significant.

A careful reading of First Samuel 16 and 17 confirms that David was not well thought of by his brothers, which gives us cause to wonder what David thought about himself. The fact is that many of us struggle to have a healthy, positive self-image for various reasons — including the negative thoughts and opinions of others. Consequently, we sometimes eliminate ourselves from being used of God because we don't think we are worthy to carry out His will for our lives.

The truth is none of us are worthy without Jesus. But through faith in Him, God made us worthy. "For He made Him [Jesus] who knew no sin to be sin for us, that we might become the righteousness of God in Him" (2 Corinthians 5:21).

Friend, God does not see as man sees. Instead of focusing on outward appearance and performance as people do, the Lord looks at the heart (*see* 1 Samuel 16:7).

Anyone can be used of God! You don't have to have a lot of education or a lot of money. You don't need to be handsome or beautiful by the world's standards. All you need is to be *in Christ Jesus*. It is Who is inside you that makes you worthy and able to accomplish God's will in your life.

When God looked at David, He saw a man after His own heart. He saw all the makings of a giant killer and a king for His people. Likewise, when God looks at you, He sees a giant killer on the inside! He sees you filled with His Holy Spirit, having all the makings of a mighty warrior ready to do His will.

Battlelines Were Drawn
Between Israel and the Philistines

Time passed, and the army of Israel was now involved in a standoff with the army of the Philistines in the Valley of Elah. The Bible states that for 40 days, the Philistines sent out their biggest and fiercest champion to intimidate and taunt the Israelites every morning and every evening, blaspheming God and cursing the people of Israel. That champion was a giant named Goliath from the city of Gath.

At that time, Jesse's three oldest sons — Eliab, Abinadab, and Shammah — had followed Saul into battle and were encamped in the Valley of Elah. Wanting to find out how they were doing, the Bible says, "...Jesse said to his son David, 'Take now for your brothers an ephah of this dried grain and these ten loaves, and run to your brothers at the camp. And carry these ten cheeses to the captain of their thousand, and see how your brothers fare, and bring back news of them'" (1 Samuel 17:17-18).

When David arrived at the encampment to see his brothers, Goliath came forward to curse the army of Israel and blaspheme the Lord just as he had done so many times before — and David heard him. David also overheard the tremendous reward being offered by the king to any man who killed Goliath — great riches, a lifetime of tax exemption, and the hand of the king's daughter in marriage.

The Bible tells us, "...David spoke to the men who stood by him, saying, 'What shall be done for the man who kills this Philistine and takes away the reproach from Israel? For who is this uncircumcised Philistine, that he should defy the armies of the living God?'" (1 Samuel 17:26). After hearing the details of the reward a second time, David began to believe that he would be the one to take out the giant and receive the prize being offered by the king.

When Eliab Opposed David,
David Turned to Another

Of course, to be a giant killer, you will have to face opposition. As strange as it may seem, the first opposition that came against David was from his own family. The Bible says:

> **Now Eliab his oldest brother heard when he spoke to the men; and Eliab's anger was aroused against David, and he said, "Why did you come down here? And with whom have you left those few sheep in the wilderness? I know your pride and the insolence of your heart, for you have come down to see the battle."**
> **— 1 Samuel 17:28**

Can you imagine! There David was trying to rid Israel of the terrorizing giant Goliath, and his own brother began to cut him down, belittling him by saying he only had a "few sheep" to care for, and calling David proudful and brazenly disrespectful.

How did David respond when his older brother came against him? The Bible tells us that David said, "'…What have I done now? Is there not a cause?' Then he turned from him toward another…" (1 Samuel 17:29).

The truth is, when God gives you an assignment, not everyone is going to get excited and support you and believe in your dream or vision. Like David, when people attack you or try to discourage you, just do what he did — *turn toward another*. Don't argue with your accuser and don't agree with them. Simply turn toward others who will support you and believe in you.

When Saul Doubted David, David Respectfully Reviewed His Own Past Victories

Continuing on with this story, the Bible says that David's interaction with the soldiers on the frontline were reported to King Saul, and Saul sent for him.

> **Then David said to Saul, "Let no man's heart fail because of him; your servant will go and fight with this Philistine." And Saul said to David, "You are not able to go against this Philistine to fight with him; for you are a youth, and he a man of war from his youth."**
> **— 1 Samuel 17:32-33**

Here we see a second wave of opposition David faced in his effort to become a giant killer. This time, it came from the highest authority in the land — King Saul himself. Basically, Saul told David, "You are not able. You're too young and inexperienced. You don't have what it takes to get the job done."

How did David respond to the king's doubt-filled reprimand? The Bible says:

> **David said to Saul, "Your servant used to keep his father's sheep, and when a lion or a bear came and took a lamb out of the flock, I went out after it and struck it, and delivered the lamb from its mouth; and when it arose against me, I caught it by its beard, and struck and killed it. Your servant has killed both lion and bear; and this uncircumcised Philistine will be like one of them, seeing he has defied the armies of the living God." Moreover David said, "The Lord, who delivered me from the paw of the lion and from the paw of the bear, He will deliver me from the hand of this Philistine...."**
> **— 1 Samuel 17:34-37**

In these verses, David essentially told Saul, "I respect you and what you're saying. But I want you to know what I've already faced and what I've already defeated as I shepherded my father's flock. God helped me defeat both lion and bear, and this uncircumcised Philistine will be like one of them."

Use Your Imagination
To Visualize Your Victory

Now, this brings us to a very important aspect of battle that doesn't get talked about much, and that is the subject of one's *imagination*. Regardless of the giant you are facing — sickness and disease, financial lack and poverty, marriage or relational challenges — what you "see" is what you're going to receive.

Like Goliath, Satan and his demons are champions at intimidation and instilling all kinds of fear. "I have the power," the enemy roars in our ears, "and you are powerless!" The enemy will do anything he can to get us to be anxious, worried, or fearful. Ultimately, his goal is to get us to visualize defeat in our situation, because *as a man thinks in his heart, so is he in reality* (*see* Proverbs 23:7).

Of all the head games Satan plays, the multiple rounds of "What If" can really wreak havoc if we give in to them. *What if this happens?* we think. *Or what if that happens? That happened to so and so, and it could happen to me too.* Our imagination, which is often rooted in carnal thinking, can certainly take us in the wrong direction.

Thankfully, we can learn to surrender our mind to the Lord and use our imagination for good. That is what David did. From the very beginning, he used his imagination to visualize his victory. You can hear it in the way he responded to all the opposition he faced.

Looking again at First Samuel 17:36 and 37, he told Saul:

> **"Your servant has killed both lion and bear; and this uncircumcised Philistine will be like one of them, seeing he has defied the armies of the living God." Moreover David said, "The Lord, who delivered me from the paw of the lion and from the paw of the bear, He will deliver me from the hand of this Philistine...."**

You can see that David carefully chose his words to paint a picture of victory. He already saw it in his mind's eye, and then he described it out loud. How did Saul respond to David's words?

> **...And Saul said to David, "Go, and the Lord be with you!"**
> **— 1 Samuel 17:37**

Friend, if you're not imagining or visualizing your victory, then by default you're imagining and visualizing your defeat. In David's mind, Goliath was already defeated, and his head was already cut off. That's the way you need to see every giant you are facing, regardless of its name!

Wear Your Own Armor, Not Someone Else's

As soon as David got the approval of the king to go against Goliath, Saul attempted to clothe David in his armor. The Bible says, "...[Saul] put a bronze helmet on his head; he also clothed him with a coat of mail. David fastened his sword to his armor and tried to walk, for he had not tested them. And David said to Saul, 'I cannot walk with these, for I have not tested them.' So David took them off" (1 Samuel 17:38-39).

Clearly, Saul and David were not the same size, so Saul's armor didn't fit David. Although Saul may have meant well, David couldn't be successful wearing the king's armor. It was too big, too heavy, and too cumbersome, and David had never tested it. David needed the protection and weaponry that best fit him.

Trying to do exactly what someone else did when they faced a similar battle is like David trying to wear Saul's armor. Although God may use the examples of other godly men and women to encourage you in your situation, He will not ask you to become a clone of someone else. He wants to walk with you and show you the best way to act in each situation you're facing.

The God we serve is very personal, and He wants you to know Him intimately. So when you're facing a giant, don't go searching for this person and that person to receive answers from them. Instead, go straight to God and say, "Father, what do *You* want me to do?" That's what David did. Basically, he told Saul, "I can't use your armor — I can't even walk in your armor."

After taking off Saul's battle gear, the Bible says, "…[David] took his staff in his hand; and he chose for himself five smooth stones from the brook, and put them in a shepherd's bag, in a pouch which he had, and his sling was in his hand. And he drew near to the Philistine" (1 Samuel 17:40).

David Defeated Goliath
Just as He Believed and Spoke

Here's the situation. David, an average-sized young man, made his way out onto the open terrain of the Valley of Elah where he met the Philistine champion Goliath of Gath. Towering nine to ten feet in height, wearing a coat of armor that weighed more than 125 pounds, the giant looked down in disbelief as David approached. The Bible says:

> **And when the Philistine looked about and saw David, he disdained him; for he was only a youth, ruddy and good-looking. So the Philistine said to David, "Am I a dog, that you come to me with sticks?" And the Philistine cursed David by his gods. And the Philistine said to David, "Come to me, and I will give your flesh to the birds of the air and the beasts of the field!"**
> **— 1 Samuel 17:42-44**

For most people, the sight of a gigantic warrior like Goliath would invoke great terror and cause one to start running in the other direction. But David was not most people. He had already defeated a lion and a bear, and he believed Goliath was simply the next in line to be conquered. Scripture tells us:

Then David said to the Philistine, "You come to me with a sword, with a spear, and with a javelin. But I come to you in the name of the Lord of hosts, the God of the armies of Israel, whom you have defied. This day the Lord will deliver you into my hand, and I will strike you and take your head from you. And this day I will give the carcasses of the camp of the Philistines to the birds of the air and the wild beasts of the earth, that all the earth may know that there is a God in Israel. Then all this assembly shall know that the Lord does not save with sword and spear; for the battle is the Lord's, and He will give you into our hands."

— 1 Samuel 17:45-47

David's declaration revealed how much confidence he had in God's ability — and you know how the story ended. David quickly ran toward the giant, grabbed a stone from his bag, put it in his sling, and flung it at Goliath's head. The rock struck the Philistine with such strong force that it sunk into his forehead, and he fell on his face to the ground. Wasting no time, David ran to Goliath, took the giant's huge sword, and cut off his head (*see* 1 Samuel 17:48-51). Thus, David prevailed in victory over the Philistine just as he had visualized and spoken out in faith before the battle began.

See Yourself as the Victor and Not the Victim

Again, Proverbs 23:7 says, "For as he [a man] thinks in his heart, so is he…." From the very beginning, David used his imagination to visualize victory. In David's mind, Goliath was already defeated, and his head was already cut off. David saw himself as the *victor*, not the victim, and that's the way you need to see yourself with every giant you face, regardless of its name.

When you were born again, you were saved in the name of Jesus, and you received the name of Jesus as a weapon you can use to defeat the enemy. His Name is the Name above every other name (*see* Philippians 2:9-11). The name of Jesus is greater than cancer and all other diseases, stronger than poverty and financial lack, and mightier than any relationship problems you may face.

David stood and declared victory over the giant "in the name of the Lord of hosts, the God of the armies of Israel." And you are to stand and declare victory over the giants you face in the mighty name of the Lord Jesus Christ! In Heaven, "...His name shall be on [our] foreheads" (Revelation 22:4). On earth, His name should be in our mouths, declaring victory over the enemy.

Remember, the Holy Spirit lives on the inside of you, and "...He who is in you is greater than he who is in the world" (1 John 4:4). It's time for the giant killer within you to stand up and conquer your giants in the mighty name of Jesus!

STUDY QUESTIONS

Be diligent to present yourself approved to God, a worker
who does not need to be ashamed, rightly dividing the word of truth.
— 2 Timothy 2:15

1. After reading through this lesson, what are some of your greatest takeaways? What is the Holy Spirit showing you about David, about Goliath, and about their epic fight? What are you learning about King Saul, Jesse, and David's brothers?

2. What "giant" are you currently facing? Are you listening to and believing its trash talk? Or are you turning a deaf ear to your giant's insults and intimidation? Consider again David's response to Goliath in First Samuel 17:45-47. What is the Holy Spirit showing you in his words? What adjustments do you need Him to help you make moving forward? Consider the attribute of God described in Romans 4:17 as you answer.

PRACTICAL APPLICATION

But be doers of the word,
and not hearers only, deceiving yourselves.
— James 1:22

1. In all honesty, how would you describe your self-image? Do you view yourself in a mostly positive way, or do you see yourself in more negative ways? How do you believe God sees you? Take some time to get alone in prayer and ask Him, "Father, how do YOU see me?" Then listen for

His voice and the impressions He puts in your spirit. Write what He tells you.

2. If you sometimes struggle with feeling worthy to carry out God's will, take some time to meditate on the following verses. They will help you realize that you are deeply loved by God, and it is because of Jesus' finished work on the Cross that we are made worthy.

- Romans 5:5-11; 8:1-3

- Ephesians 2:4-9

- 1 John 3:20-21; 4:17-19

3. When David was verbally attacked by his brother, he turned toward another. And when he faced doubt and uncertainty from King Saul, he respectfully explained how God had helped him in the past. How do you usually respond when people oppose you? What can you learn from David's example and implement in your own life? Pray and ask the Holy Spirit to help you begin to carefully choose your words to paint pictures of victory rather than defeat.

LESSON 4

TOPIC

Are You Using the Weapon of Love?

SCRIPTURES

1. **1 Corinthians 13:4-8** — Love suffers long and is kind; love does not envy; love does not parade itself, is not puffed up; does not behave rudely, does not seek its own, is not provoked, thinks no evil; does not rejoice in iniquity, but rejoices in the truth; bears all things, believes all things, hopes all things, endures all things. Love never fails....

2. **Proverbs 25:15** — By long forbearance a ruler is persuaded, and a gentle tongue breaks a bone.

3. **Proverbs 15:1** — A soft answer turns away wrath, but a harsh word stirs up anger.

4. **John 3:16** — For God so loved the world that He gave His only begotten Son, that whoever believes in Him should not perish but have everlasting life.

5. **1 John 4:18** — There is no fear in love; but perfect love casts out fear, because fear involves torment. But he who fears has not been made perfect in love.

6. **Romans 5:5** — Now hope does not disappoint, because the love of God has been poured out in our hearts by the Holy Spirit who was given to us.

7. **John 17:26** — And I have declared to them Your name, and will declare it, that the love with which You loved Me may be in them, and I in them.

8. **Ephesians 3:17** — That Christ may dwell in your hearts through faith; that you, being rooted and grounded in love....

SYNOPSIS

As we continue our study on fighting against the giants in our lives, it is important to note that when Jesus was crucified, buried, and raised from the dead, He stripped the enemy of his power. The Bible makes this clear, declaring, "[God] disarmed the principalities and powers that were ranged against us and made a bold display and public example of them, in triumphing over them in Him and in it [the cross]" (Colossians 2:15 *AMPC*).

In addition to the blood of Jesus, the name of Jesus, and God's Word, another very powerful weapon we have been given as believers is the love of God. In this lesson, we are going to see how God's indescribable love defeats fear, shuts down arguments, and opens the way to everlasting life.

The emphasis of this lesson:

God's love was poured into our hearts the moment we got saved, and it is the most powerful weapon we have against the enemy. Love manifests in countless ways, including a gentle tongue, a soft answer, and patience. Love casts out fear, gives extravagantly to others, and can transform the hardest of hearts into a lover of God.

Sharing God's Love Builds Bridges That Connect People With Jesus

The Bible says in First Corinthians 13:8 that *love never fails*, and there is a unique story about a godly man who operated in that kind of love. His name was David Wilkerson. While Wilkerson lived in Texas many decades ago, God started speaking to his heart about the gangs in New York City. Reports told of how dangerous these gangs had become — they were hurting people, robbing people, and at times even killing people.

As this godly man in Texas heard about what was going on, the Holy Spirit said to him, "I want you to go there and begin preaching to those gang members, teaching them about my great love for them."

In obedience to the Lord, Wilkerson shared his vision with people in his church, and they took up a collection to help him get to New York City. Of course, the streets were filled with deep darkness, but that didn't stop this preacher from going out and telling the gang members about Jesus.

Now there was one particular group Wilkerson met whose leader really resisted the message. As he began preaching and telling them that God loved them and Jesus loved them and died for them, the leader became vocally irate. His name was Nicky Cruz, and when the preacher told him that Jesus loved him, Nicky said, "If you tell me Jesus loves me one more time, I'm going to cut you into pieces!"

"Nicky," Wilkerson replied, "If you cut me into pieces, every piece of me will be saying the same thing — Jesus loves you, and so do I."

The Holy Spirit used this obedient man's words to melt the heart of Nicky Cruz. The love of Jesus so overwhelmed him that he couldn't resist it any longer, and he gave his life to Christ. He became a powerful evangelist that traveled the world, reaching hardcore people who were lost just like he had been and telling them about the love of Jesus.

What won Nicky and numerous other gang members to the Lord? What delivered them from a life of violence and drug addiction? It wasn't someone coming and telling them how wrong they were and that they were going to hell. Although that was certainly true, it was not the news of the impending judgment of God that saved Nicky or anyone else. It was the love of God that came pouring out of the godly man who came to New York City out of obedience to God. Love is what changed Nicky forever.

Love Speaks With
a Gentle Tongue and a Soft Answer

Friend, love is the most powerful weapon that we have against the enemy and all his assaults. The Bible has many things to say about love and all the different ways it manifests. For example, when we come to Proverbs 25:15, we learn:

By long forbearance a ruler is persuaded, and a gentle tongue breaks a bone.

Think about a *gentle tongue*. A tongue that is gentle is one that is filled with love, not criticism. A gentle tongue is not trying to get even with others, prove a point, or show that it is right. A gentle tongue is patient, slow to speak, and slow to get angry. That kind of tongue speaks loving words that the Bible says can "break a bone." In other words, a gentle tongue that speaks the truth in love is so powerful it can break through even the hardest hearts of people and difficult situations.

Think about it. What kind of speech comes out of your mouth — especially when someone attacks you or a loved one? Is it patient? Is it kind? If it is, it's going to "break the bone" and eventually cause the hardness in that person to soften and be broken so that true healing can take place.

We find a similar truth in Proverbs 15:1, where it says:

A soft answer turns away wrath, but a harsh word stirs up anger.

Harsh words are unloving words, which act like gasoline poured on a fire. They lead to enflamed, out-of-control emotions that will burn down relationships. Soft words, on the other hand, are loving words that are like water poured on the fire of wrath to extinguish it. If someone is angry with you, saying words that are rude, cruel, and hurtful, and you answer that person softly, his anger will be diffused.

Where do we get a soft answer with which to respond to others? It comes from a strong position of love. When a person comes at you with harsh, angry words and you speak a soft answer in reply, it means you don't give back the same anger, the same criticism, or the same hate they gave you. Likewise, a soft answer, like a gentle tongue, does not withdraw one's heart or aim to get even with someone.

A soft answer will absolutely rebuke and stop wrath. Wrath will have to bow its knee and take a back seat to a soft answer. Yes, friend, a heart filled with the love of God will produce a mouth filled with loving words — including a gentle tongue and a soft answer — powerful weapons that are undefeatable.

Love Gives Extravagantly
and Love Casts Out Fear

There is no greater love than the love that comes from God. Not only is it unconditional, but it is also powerfully motivating. It was the intense, immeasurable love of God that drove Him to save us from sin by sending Jesus to die in our place. The Bible declares:

> **For God so loved the world that He gave His only begotten Son, that whoever believes in Him should not perish but have everlasting life.**
>
> **— John 3:16**

God's love is in a category all its own, and it is unstoppable and undefeatable! It's that kind of love that Jesus displayed in His selfless sacrifice to save us, heal us, and deliver us from the powers of darkness. That's the kind of love that's on the inside of you, which we'll talk more about in a moment.

Something else that love does is that it completely deals with fear. The Bible tells us in First John 4:18:

> **There is no fear in love; but perfect love casts out fear, because fear involves torment. But he who fears has not been made perfect in love.**

Love is so powerful that it will *cast out*, *push out*, and *evict* fear. It will put fear down, rebuke fear, and cause fear to run from us.

One trusted commentary says that "perfect love casting out fear" is a picture of *disciplinary action*. It's like having an angry dog that wants to bite you, and you take a position of authority and say, "No! Stop it, right now! You're not biting anyone!" When that dog hears your tone and sees the fierceness in your eyes, it will back down and retreat in fear because it's been disciplined. That is a picture of how love stands in complete authority over fear and puts it in its place.

You Have God's Love
Inside You!

Now you may be thinking, *Where in the world do I get this love?* The answer is simple — it comes from God. God IS love (*see* 1 John 4:8,16). Love is not just something God does — it is who He is! And if you are a born-again child of God, His love is living on the inside of you!

Writing under the anointing of the Holy Spirit, the apostle Paul declared:

> **...The love of God has been poured out in our hearts by the Holy Spirit who was given to us.**
> **— Romans 5:5**

What is most amazing about the love of God that's been poured into our hearts is that it is the exact same love with which the Father loves Jesus. It is not a lesser, "junior-sized" love or a smaller sample of God's love. It is the exact same, full-blown love the Father has for Jesus. This truth is confirmed by Jesus Himself in His final prayer for all His followers just before going to the Cross. He said:

> **And I [Jesus] have declared to them Your name, and will declare it, that** *the love with which You loved Me may be in them*, **and I in them.**
> **— John 17:26**

Isn't that magnificent! The exact same measure and quality of love that the Father has for His Son Jesus, He has for YOU! And He poured that love inside you in the Person of the Holy Spirit the very moment you repented of your sin and welcomed Jesus to be your Lord and Savior. In that moment, you became armed with a weapon that no enemy can stand against!

Olga's Story of Transforming Love

The Bible says that one of the ways we overcome the enemy is through sharing our testimony (*see* Revelation 12:11). Denise told an amazing story of a lady named Olga who was a leader in her women's ministry many years ago in another part of the world. It seemed that every time Olga walked into their meetings, she carried herself like a beautiful princess. Her shoulders were back, her head was held high, and her apparel was exquisite.

Deeply intrigued, Denise and several of the leaders took the opportunity one day to ask Olga why she looked so put together every time she came to their gatherings and why she always carried herself like a princess. Here is what Olga shared:

To understand my story, you need to know that my mother was very abusive. She beat me so much that I would bleed and have cuts on my body. It was terrible and caused many psychological problems. In fact, the way I was treated was so horrific I became paralyzed all over my body and bound to a wheelchair.

Many of my relatives and friends began to tell me, 'You need to just give up.' In those days, public places weren't very accommodating or friendly to those in wheelchairs. Today, people can get around much easier than back then. Most people who were confined to wheelchairs and couldn't walk just stayed in their apartment.

But I was only 21 years old, and I really didn't want to die. In spite of all I had been through, I had a will to live.

Well, living in the next apartment was a woman who had just been saved, filled with the Holy Spirit, and set on fire for God. The Holy Spirit spoke to her and said, 'I want you to go next door to your neighbor's house because there's someone there you need to pray for.'

In obedience to God, she came over with the boldness of a lion and found me sitting in my wheelchair. Immediately, she knew in her spirit, *This is the one I am to pray for.* As she continued listening to the Holy Spirit, He instructed her to take some water and pour it on the top of my head and let it run all the way down my body, and that is exactly what she did.

That water drenched my hair, went down my shoulders, and covered my body, and as it did, the power of God touched me and miraculously healed me!

Now, you'd think, *That's fantastic! What a great story!* And it certainly is, but that is not the end of it. Although God did supernaturally heal me at age 21, I did not give my life to the Lord at that time. Instead, I fell in love with a man I met, and we began living together. We soon had a daughter, and things were going pretty good in the beginning. But then he started to drink, stopped going to work, and cussed me out every day. My heart became so broken that it's hard to describe.

I remember taking a calendar and checking off each day that he came home drunk. Day after day, month after month, the calendar was filled with a record of his drunkenness. Finally, I said to myself, *I don't know what to do with this man. He has hurt me so deeply, and I have no hope for him changing.*

Around that time, someone invited me to church, and I went and gave my life to Jesus. When I went back home, I told the man I was living with, 'I am not married to you, so I cannot sleep with you anymore.' And I moved to another room in the house.

Still brokenhearted, I began to wonder and pray, *What am I going to do with this horrible man?* Then the Holy Spirit spoke to me and gave me a strategy. He said, 'Tonight, when he comes home, your weapon is *love*. That's how you're going to pull this giant down! I want you to dress in your best dress, make his favorite food, and when he comes through that door, I want you to say, "Oh my love. You've come home."'

In obedience, I did exactly what the Holy Spirit told me to do. Again and again, he would come in late, be drunk and smelly, and treat me rudely. Yet, I presented myself like a princess and served him delicious food. Days, weeks, and months passed, and I continued doing exactly what God had told me.

Amazingly, after two years, he got saved! He then married me and adopted our daughter. He also quit drinking and got a job. The love of God transformed that man and my life, and that is why I continue to carry myself as a princess everywhere I go.

Think about it. Would a constant flow of criticism, anger, words of hate, and threats of "I'm leaving you" ever have changed that man? No, not at all. The thing that changed him was the weapon of unconditional love — the love of God that had been shed abroad in Olga's heart by the Holy Spirit the day she got saved. That same supernatural love of God is inside you, and with the empowering strength of the Holy Spirit, it can become a weapon to pull down the giants you're facing in your life.

Get Rooted in God's Love

Friend, receiving, understanding, and walking in love is so important for us as believers. That is why the Holy Spirit moved on the apostle Paul to pray, "That Christ may dwell in your hearts through faith; that you, [are] being rooted and grounded in love" (Ephesians 3:17). God wants us to be deeply rooted in His love.

When we hear the word *roots*, we often think about trees, and there are several species that are known for having the deepest root systems in the world. These include white oaks, hickories, walnuts, and wild fig trees, which have been found to have roots reaching more than 300 feet in depth.[1] Trees with deep roots are difficult to blow over and stand strong even in the most violent storms.

In the same way, the deeper our roots are in God's love, the stronger we are to weather life's storms. His Holy Spirit living in us will enable us to love people unconditionally, give them mercy, and not treat them like the rest of the world would. Aren't you grateful that God doesn't give us what we deserve? Because of Jesus, He forgives us and gives us new mercy every morning (*see* Lamentations 3:22-23).

Remember that no foe can stand against the power of love. It is a weapon you have to defeat the enemy. It will overcome things like fear, doubt, hate, betrayal, denial, and false accusations. When you give others the love of God that's on the inside of you, you give them the very power and presence of God, and "Love never fails…" (1 Corinthians 13:8). It is the weapon no enemy can withstand!

STUDY QUESTIONS

Be diligent to present yourself approved to God, a worker
who does not need to be ashamed, rightly dividing the word of truth.
— 2 Timothy 2:15

1. First Corinthians 13 is known as the "love chapter," and verses 4 through 8 are very specific. This section depicts how God loves you and how we are to love others by His grace. As you take time to slowly meditate on this passage, what is the Holy Spirit showing you about the love God gives to you every moment of every day? Where do you really need Him to help you come up higher in your love toward others?

2. One of the greatest prayers you can pray regularly is to have a deeper revelation of God's love for you. The apostle Paul actually prays this for the believers in Ephesians 3:16-21. Take time to reflect on this

powerful passage in a few different Bible versions, and in your own words create a personalized prayer, asking God to give you a greater understanding of His love.

PRACTICAL APPLICATION

But be doers of the word,
and not hearers only, deceiving yourselves.
—James 1:22

1. We know from Romans 5:5 that the love of God was poured into our heart the moment we got saved. The question is, *how does God's love grow*? Carefully read First John 4:11-19 and describe the conditions that are needed to experience God's love increasing and becoming more and more complete within you.

2. A *gentle tongue* that speaks the truth in love is so powerful it can break through even the hardest hearts of people and tough situations. Can you remember a time in which someone spoke to you *gently*, giving you *a soft answer* when you were harsh with him or her? How did it affect you? Have you ever given someone a soft answer when that person was harsh with you? How did it affect the situation?

------

[1]Laoluwah, "10 Tree Species With The Deepest Roots," SafeAndSanitaryHomes, January 1, 2024, https://www.safeandsanitaryhomes.org/tree-with-deepest-roots. Accessed March 25, 2025.

TOPIC

Is Complaining the Giant in Your Life?

SCRIPTURES

1. **Numbers 14:1-4** — So all the congregation lifted up their voices and cried, and the people wept that night. And all the children of Israel complained against Moses and Aaron, and the whole congregation said to them, "If only we had died in the land of Egypt! Or if only we had died in this wilderness! Why has the Lord brought us to this land to fall by the sword, that our wives and children should become victims? Would it not be better for us to return to Egypt?" So they said to one another, "Let us select a leader and return to Egypt."

2. **Numbers 14:27** — How long shall I bear with this evil congregation who complain against Me? I have heard the complaints which the children of Israel make against Me.

3. **Hebrews 3:8-9** — Do not harden your hearts as in the rebellion, in the day of trial in the wilderness, where your fathers tested Me, tried Me, and saw My works forty years.

4. **Philippians 1:3** — I thank my God upon every remembrance of you.

5. **Philippians 4:18** — Indeed I have all and abound. I am full, having received from Epaphroditus the things sent from you, a sweet-smelling aroma, an acceptable sacrifice, well pleasing to God.

SYNOPSIS

One of the giants all of us face is *complaining*. When things don't go our way or bad things happen that we have not planned, our natural response is to complain. Indeed, complaining is a giant problem in our world, and it is so easy to be taken captive by it.

Nevertheless, the Bible says, "Do all things *without* grumbling and faultfinding and complaining [against God] and questioning and doubting [among yourselves]" (Philippians 2:14 *AMPC*). How can we escape the snare of complaining? By cultivating a thankful heart.

The emphasis of this lesson:

Complaining is a giant problem with dangerous results. The nation of Israel serves as our example to not complain. When we're dissatisfied with what is going on in our lives, instead of complaining, we must choose to be thankful and purposely express our thanks to God for all He has done and what He is doing.

Complaining Is Dangerous

The word "complaining" is defined as *murmuring, an expression of dissatisfaction*, or *grumbling*. It describes *muttering in a low voice* or *a grumbling action that promotes ill will instead of harmony and goodwill*. It also denotes *inward questioning, argued discussion*, or *skeptical questioning and criticism*. It refers to *intellectual rebellion against God*.

When we complain, we are basically criticizing God, telling Him, "I don't like what You're doing in my life, and if I were in control, things would be different." The Bible is filled with examples of the consequences of complaining. This is especially clear in the lives of the Israelites when they first came out of Egypt.

The People of Israel Had a Bad Habit of Complaining

A careful study of Israel's exodus from slavery shows the mighty hand of God working powerfully on their behalf. God not only brought them out of captivity, but also rescued them from their enemies in the following situations:

- The Israelites watched as God brought ten supernatural plagues on their Egyptian captors.
- The Israelites saw the Red Sea part, allowing them to walk through it on dry ground.
- The Israelites witnessed those walls of water collapse and drown the Egyptians in the sea behind them.
- The Israelites were supernaturally guided and protected by a cloud during the day and a pillar of fire at night as they walked through the wilderness.

God also miraculously provided an abundance of water from a rock in the desert and a bread-like substance called *manna*, which rained daily from the sky as their food. In fact, when we calculate how much manna God caused to pour from the windows of Heaven over the 40 years that the Israelites were in the wilderness, we discover that approximately 65,700,000 tons of manna were provided!

Yet, despite all these unbelievable miracles, the people began to regularly complain — especially over the manna. The Bible says:

> **Now the mixed multitude who were among them yielded to intense craving; so the children of Israel also wept again and said: "Who will give us meat to eat? We remember the fish which we ate freely in Egypt, the cucumbers, the melons, the leeks, the onions, and the garlic; but now our whole being is dried up; there is nothing at all except this manna before our eyes!"**
>
> **— Numbers 11:4-6**

In frustration, Moses cried out to God, and God answered him. He told Moses to have the people consecrate themselves because He was going to give them the meat they were craving and longing to receive. Then the Lord caused a wind to bring quail from the sea all around the camp of Israel. He did this for an entire month. Researchers calculate that about 90 million quail showed up every day for one month, and the people ate quail until it came out of their noses, and they were sick of it (*see* Numbers 11:20).

Complaining Kept the Israelites From Entering the Promised Land

Unfortunately, the Israelites did not learn their lesson and stop complaining. In fact, complaining had become such a bad habit that when it was finally time for them to enter the Promised Land, their complaining prevented them from doing so.

Before entering the land of Canaan, Moses was instructed by the Lord to send 12 leaders from Israel, one man from each tribe to survey and spy out the land. After 40 days of traveling through the territory and observing things, the spies returned — and 10 of them had an evil report. The Bible says:

> **…The men who had gone up with him said, "We are not able to go up against the people, for they are stronger than we." And they gave the children of Israel a bad report of the land which**

they had spied out, saying, "The land through which we have gone as spies is a land that devours its inhabitants, and all the people whom we saw in it are men of great stature. There we saw the giants (the descendants of Anak came from the giants); and we were like grasshoppers in our own sight, and so we were in their sight."

— Numbers 13:31-33

Only two of the spies — Joshua from the tribe of Benjamin and Caleb from the tribe of Issachar — gave a positive, faith-filled report to the people. They said, "…The land we passed through to spy out is an exceedingly good land. If the Lord delights in us, then He will bring us into this land and give it to us, 'a land which flows with milk and honey.' Only do not rebel against the Lord, nor fear the people of the land, for they are our bread; their protection has departed from them, and the Lord is with us. Do not fear them" (Numbers 14:7-9).

But the Israelites believed and received the bad report of the ten spies instead of the good report of Joshua and Caleb, and the Bible says in Numbers 14:1-4:

So all the congregation lifted up their voices and cried, and the people wept that night. And all the children of Israel complained against Moses and Aaron, and the whole congregation said to them, "If only we had died in the land of Egypt! Or if only we had died in this wilderness! Why has the Lord brought us to this land to fall by the sword, that our wives and children should become victims? Would it not be better for us to return to Egypt?" So they said to one another, "Let us select a leader and return to Egypt."

Once the people of Israel believed the negative report, they began to grumble and complain, and they became deceived by their complaining. That is what complaining does — it *deceives* us. It tricks us into thinking we have a right to complain and that we are right in our complaining.

The Israelites were so deceived that they thought they would be better off returning to Egypt. They were so mixed up in their thinking that going back into bondage and slavery appeared better than moving forward on God's word to take the land.

God Takes Complaining Personally

At that point, God had had enough of the Israelites' murmuring and complaining. The Bible says, "…The Lord spoke to Moses and Aaron, saying, 'How long shall I bear with this evil congregation who complain against Me? I have heard the complaints which the children of Israel make against Me" (Numbers 14:26-27).

Notice that God said the people were complaining *against Him*. When we are dissatisfied with what is going on in our life and we complain about our circumstances, our situations, or people we encounter, God takes it personally. He sees our complaints as against Him, which is the last thing any of us would want.

Complaining is so repulsive to God that He warns us against it in the New Testament. Referring to the story of the Israelites, the writer of Hebrews tells us, "Do not harden your hearts as in the rebellion, in the day of trial in the wilderness, where your fathers tested Me, tried Me, and saw My works forty years" (Hebrews 3:8-9).

Here we see clearly that complaining will *harden our hearts*, which is why we cannot let the giant of complaining have rulership over our life. Instead, we must obediently cooperate with the Holy Spirit and keep our hearts soft and sensitive to His voice.

Complaining Can Ruin a Marriage

One area where complaining has caused devastating effects is in marriage. Sadly, many marriages are severely damaged by spouses that constantly complain. This is especially true of wives who have an attitude of complaining about numerous things. They don't like how their husband treats their mother or that the children don't get enough of their father's time and attention. They murmur that their husband doesn't make enough money and complain about how he eats and leaves his dirty clothes on the floor.

On the other hand, there are some husbands who complain and say their wife is always spending too much money, doesn't take care of the house, and is always on social media. Others complain of a lack of attention and a lack of desire for sexual intimacy. Continual complaining in a marriage from either spouse can build a wall so thick that the sweet communication the husband and wife once shared is lost. In the most severe cases, complaining has even brought some marriages to the place of divorce.

As wives and husbands, we must be careful not to let that giant of complaining overcome us and harden our hearts. This is especially true for us as ladies, as statistics show women have a greater tendency to give in to complaining. Nevertheless, we all need to humble ourselves before God and receive His grace to walk in love, looking for and believing the best of our spouse. With the help of the Holy Spirit, we can learn to take the high road, cultivating an attitude of gratitude and praying for our spouse instead of complaining about them.

Paul Chose To Be Thankful Despite Dire Circumstances

So how can we take down the giant of complaining? It is through *thankfulness*. The apostle Paul's life is an amazing example of being thankful in the midst of dreadful circumstances. This seems to shine most vividly in his attitude and actions while suffering in a Roman prison.

Historians tell us that when Paul wrote the book of Philippians, he was incarcerated in a terrible place. Unlike many of today's jails that are equipped with air conditioning, televisions, and places to exercise, the prison where Paul and others were incarcerated was below the city, and it also served as a holding tank for the sewage from the palace above. Historians also say that rats were crawling on the raw sewage Paul was standing in and that people were dying all around him.

It was in that dark and horrible environment that Paul wrote the book of Philippians. Amazingly, he began his writing, saying, "I *thank* my God upon every remembrance of you" (Philippians 1:3). Rather than complain about the wretched conditions and death that surrounded him on every side, Paul chose to be thankful. Wow!

Then in Philippians 4:18, he went on to say, "Indeed I have all and abound. I am full, having received from Epaphroditus the things sent from you, a sweet-smelling aroma, an acceptable sacrifice, well pleasing to God." In that terrible place, Paul focused on what God had provided him through the Philippian believers, and he chose to be thankful! He said, "I have all and abound." How could he abound in that horrible prison? He did it by choosing to be thankful.

Being Thankful Produces
Indescribable Blessings

In the program, Denise shared how the testimonies of two missionaries powerfully impacted her life. The first came from a man who had been serving in the mission field for many years and had dedicated his life for the cause of Christ. After a long period of time, he was experiencing pain all over his body and was extremely exhausted from all his efforts in serving. Yet, there was one thing on his body that didn't hurt him, and it was his ears.

Having learned the importance of thanksgiving, this man of God began thanking the Lord that his ears didn't hurt. Although his circumstances didn't change, when he started thanking God, his whole demeanor was transformed. Hope filled his heart, and peace filled his mind. That is the indescribable blessing that comes from being thankful.

Another missionary, whom Denise had the privilege of meeting, had given his life to sharing the Gospel and advancing God's Kingdom in more than one country. Tragically, while he was abroad, he received news that his wife and two of his children in America were killed instantly in a car accident. Immediately, he returned to the States to grieve the loss of his loved ones and have a funeral in their honor.

Needless to say, he became so deeply depressed that he could hardly lift his head. His trust in God had been shattered. *How could God not protect my family*, he questioned within himself repeatedly. *I gave my life in other lands for the cause of Christ, and yet I lost my family. Why God? Why did You allow this to happen?*

Overwhelmed by depression and searching for answers, this missionary went to another godly minister for help. Understanding the missionary's deep pain, the minister respectfully said, "What you need is some thanksgiving. As difficult as your circumstances are, you've got to look for things for which to be thankful and express them to God."

The missionary said it took him two hours just to get one tiny word of thanksgiving out of his mouth. But voicing that one small word of thanks unlocked something in his heart, and he began to thank God freely, saying things like, "God, I thank You that I'm alive. Thank You for my salvation.

Thank You that You're in me. Thank You for Your faithfulness and for Your grace and love."

Once he started thanking God, it was like a river of thankfulness broke free on the inside of his spirit, and it flooded out of him. Little by little, all the oppression and depression he had been under lifted off of him. Eventually, that man of God got married again, had another baby, and went back to serve on the mission field. Years later, he died after having achieved a great victory in the faith.

What stopped the giant of complaining? What defeated the enemy of oppression and depression? It was *thanksgiving.*

Thank God On Purpose

Friend, complaining deceives us and blinds us to the blessings God has provided. When we become trapped in a cycle of complaining, we can no longer see and appreciate what God *has done* or what He *is doing.* Although all of us go through very disappointing situations and at times endure very difficult circumstances for which we could easily complain, we must learn to push past the tendency of complaining and look for things to thank God for on purpose.

If you're struggling through some tough times right now, go to God and tell Him. Say, "Lord, everything is not how I want it to be, and I am frustrated with [*name anything specific you're dealing with*]. But I know that You are faithful, God, and You love me. You have given me breath in my lungs and a heartbeat in my chest. You've given me a home to live in, food to eat, and a job where I can work. And Your Holy Spirit lives on the inside of me! Thank You, Father, for all You have done and are doing in my life!"

With the help of the Holy Spirit, you can choose to give thanks in all things as it says in First Thessalonians 5:18. Thankfulness will defeat the giant of complaining and transform your life in wonderful ways. So "Enter into His gates with thanksgiving, and into His courts with praise. Be thankful to Him, and bless His name" (Psalm 100:4)!

STUDY QUESTIONS

Be diligent to present yourself approved to God, a worker
who does not need to be ashamed, rightly dividing the word of truth.
— 2 Timothy 2:15

1. The importance of *not* complaining is so vital that the Holy Spirit prompted the writer of Hebrews to restate the warning in his New Testament letter. Take some time to carefully read what he wrote in the book of Hebrews chapters 3 and 4 and ponder the following questions.
   - What was God talking about when He said, "Don't harden your heart"?
   - What causes our heart to become hard? (*See* Hebrews 3:12.)
   - What blessings do we forfeit when we "harden our hearts"? (*See* Hebrews 3:11,18; 4:6.)
   - Instead of hardening our heart, what does God say we're to do? (*See* Hebrews 3:12-13; 4:1-3.)
2. Cultivating a thankful heart produces contentment in our life. What can you learn about the value of godly contentment from First Timothy 6:6-11; Hebrews 13:5-6; and Philippians 4:11-13?

PRACTICAL APPLICATION

But be doers of the word,
and not hearers only, deceiving yourselves.
— James 1:22

1. Complaining can cripple and even crush our relationships. If you're married, how would you describe the overall quality of your marriage? When you think about and talk to your spouse, are your words filled more with *complaining* or *complimenting*? When was the last time you told him or her how much you sincerely appreciate them and named specific things for which you're thankful?
2. Now take these same questions and apply them to your children, your parents, your leaders, your friends, and God. In what specific areas do you really need more of His grace and wisdom to help you stop complaining and start vocalizing sincere thankfulness?
3. Pray and ask the Holy Spirit to show you practical steps you can take to cultivate an attitude of gratitude toward God, your spouse, your children, and all the people in your life. Likewise, ask Him for the grace to put these actions into practice. If you humbly ask Him for help, He will give it to you (*see* James 4:6; 1 Peter 5:5).

A Prayer To Receive Salvation

If you've never received Jesus as your Savior and Lord, now is the time for you to experience the new life Jesus wants to give you! To receive God's gift of salvation that can be obtained through Jesus alone, pray this prayer from your heart:

Jesus, I repent of my sin and receive You as my Savior and Lord. Wash away my sin with Your precious blood and make me completely new. I thank You that my sin is removed, and Satan no longer has any right to lay claim on me. Through Your empowering grace, I faithfully promise that I will serve You as my Lord for the rest of my life.

If you just prayed this prayer of salvation, you are born again! You are a brand-new creation in Christ! Would you please let us know of your decision by going to **renner.org/salvation**? We would love to connect with you and pray for you as you begin your new life in Christ.

Scriptures for further study: John 3:16; John 14:6; Acts 4:12; Ephesians 1:7; Hebrews 10:19,20; 1 Peter 1:18,19; Romans 10:9,10; Colossians 1:13; 2 Corinthians 5:17; Romans 6:4; 1 Peter 1:3

Notes

CLAIM YOUR FREE RESOURCE!

As a way of introducing you further to the teaching ministry of Rick Renner, we would like to send you FREE of charge his teaching, "How To Receive a Miraculous Touch From God" on CD or as an MP3 download.

In His earthly ministry, Jesus commonly healed *all* who were sick of *all* their diseases. In this profound message, learn about the manifold dimensions of Christ's wisdom, goodness, power, and love toward all humanity who came to Him in faith with their needs.

☑ **YES, I want to receive Rick Renner's monthly teaching letter!**

Simply scan the QR code to claim this resource or go to: **renner.org/claim-your-free-offer**

Connect

WITH US!

 renner.org

 facebook.com/rickrenner • facebook.com/rennerdenise

 youtube.com/rennerministries • youtube.com/deniserenner

 instagram.com/rickrrenner • instagram.com/rennerministries_
 instagram.com/rennerdenise

www.ingramcontent.com/pod-product-compliance
Lightning Source LLC
Chambersburg PA
CBHW071644040426
42452CB00009B/1758